A Book of Bread

A Book of Bread

Bruce Meyer

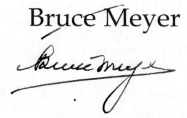

EXILE
editions

Library and Archives Canada Cataloguing in Publication

Meyer, Bruce, 1957-
    A book of bread / Bruce Meyer.

Poems.
ISBN 978-1-55096-263-5

    I. Title.

PS8576.E93B66 2011   C811'.54   C2011-907973-9

Design and Composition by Hourglass Angels~mc
Typeset in Constantia at the Moons of Jupiter Studios
Printed by Imprimerie Gauvin

Published by Exile Editions Ltd.
144483 Southgate Road 14 – GD
Holstein, Ontario, N0G 2A0
Canada   www.ExileEditions.com
Printed and Bound in Canada in 2011

Conseil des Arts   Canada Council
du Canada   for the Arts

Canadä

ONTARIO ARTS COUNCIL
CONSEIL DES ARTS DE L'ONTARIO

The publisher would like to acknowledge the financial support of the
Canada Council for the Arts, the Government of Canada through the
Canada Book Fund (CBF), and the Ontario Arts Council–an agency
of the Government of Ontario, for our publishing activities.

Sales / Distribution:
Independent Publishers Group
814 North Franklin Street, Chicago, IL 60610 USA
www.ipgbook.com   toll free: 1 800 888 4741

This book is for

Kerry, Katie, Margaret, and Carolyn

THE RECIPE

I

A Common Banquet: Autumn Chant

II

Bread: A Mass for Voices at the Winter Solstice

III

The Bread of Angels: A Spring Canticle

IV

Stone Bread: Summer Plainsong

Oh, blessed are those who sit at that table where the Bread of Angels is eaten... they who are fed at that high table are full of mercy towards those whom they see straying in one pasture with the creatures who eat grass and acorns... Wherefore, now wishing to prepare for them, I mean to make a common Banquet of this which I have shown to them, and of that needed bread without which food such as this could not be eaten by them at their feast; bread fit for such meat, which I know, without it, would be furnished forth in vain.

—DANTE, Il Convito

I

A Common Banquet: Autumn Chant

With every breath in prayer, we are more
and more akin to the bread we eat.

—BERNARD OF CLAIRVAUX

Toronto Women's Cookbook, 1873

Here is the recipe for Eve's pudding:
apples, cinnamon, and mortal temptation.

The cure for ringworm is penny mold
skimmed from the minisci of vinegar jars

as if someone knew it possessed a magic.
Take in the nose of the common home:

a man's sweat still in bed, the call of baking,
and woodsmoke from an iron stove—

there has to be a cure for every love
and for there to be beauty in domestic bliss

throw open wide all the weighted sashes
as soon as he departs at daybreak,

and dangling from the open frame—shout!
(so no one hears) all your risen heart can sing.

Fresh from the Oven
  for Katie

Though half-baked places
do not speak to the nose,
I should tell you every city
has an aroma all its own.

My nursery was in Toronto:
the smell of highways,
silos of loading wheat,
a rancid lake and its history.

London headed diesel fumes,
escalator gear-grease, urine,
beer, and stale cigarettes:
the smell of learning poetry.

New York was all adventure;
film canisters, traffic exhaust,
salt water, Lucky Strikes,
rusty steel, and an April day.

My nose followed to Boston
echoing a fishy bouquet,
salt urchin pungency, grass,
tree bark after a June rain.

Your mother and I in Chicago,
a first weekend without you,
concrete, the absence of talc,
piggies going toeless to market...

and when I kissed your head
to say goodbye, rainforests,
the New Jerusalem of bread,
fresh, warm, like coming home.

East-facing Cottage

When it cracks rain,
rice must do its magic.
Finger-coloured grains,
belonging to some stoic

eastern memory, drink
the salt shaker clean
as sun-bleached rock
flooded over an eon.

If you could hold
each crystal to a candle
you would behold
a prism or the miracle

of light inside waiting
to leap out on fracture.
My father rubbing
two sugar cubes together

in the closet as fissures
of sweet became daybreak—
he was a wizard of pure
energy—and every spark

leapt clear like a soul
on a de-fib stretcher,
the way a saltine stole
rain in a sugar dispenser.

Summma

for Thomas Aquinas

He was pouring over his midmorning muffin
when I slowly opened the door and disturbed
the angelic silence. He did not look up, nor

would he need to acknowledge my presence
for I was nothing but a single infinite point
waiting for the head of a rather unsteady

pin that held a white rose in his scholar's cap.
I thought, this is the one place where I am,
infinite made finite by simply being. Outside,

students were making a ruckus, shouting
something incredible and inaudible, but not
being there, being here among the *memento*

mori and the quills, the ink pots and cups
no one had come to collect from the clutter
of his desk, I did not have the pleasure of

omniscience. God must enjoy everything we
do because he can perceive it as a ballet
where a single instant is but a series of leaps

and bounds as incredible and stunning as
rain falling softly on the shoulders of the quad
or the night creeping painfully as death

from the edges of the city, cooling the heart.
There was sound as he cleared his throat,
and I thought, yes, he must be ready for me

now that I have made the hair stand up
on the unshaven brush land of his neck, but
it was merely a tickle in his throat, perhaps

a colleague he had swallowed earlier, my fore-
bear whose replacement seemed so necessary
for the weight of the world in a single question.

How many angels could dance on the head
of a pin? The pointy part, not the flattened
knob against which a tailor presses his tough

fingertips as he tries to piece together the fabric
of reality and time and being into one trim
hair shirt of impossibility the way a mind comes

to terms with memories and sequences of time
that cannot be contained in a single thought
yet are lived by a single mind. And as a voice

from heaven announced a banquet, there I sat
waiting for that moment when the temporal
and the eternal would intersect, communicate

with awe and reverence for the first time since
Eden and splendor of deathlessness and simple
grace, that shaking of hands across the void

of hope and hopelessness when the fingertips
of the Almighty do not seem long enough to do
what is requested of them in prayer, the frail

human desire to overcome frail human desire,
to leap like a spark from a blacksmith's anvil
into the darkness of the shodding stall and ignite

that instant recognition that all possibilities
are but illuminations waiting for the pity of vision
and beyond that there is only the will to know—

in that instant resides the purpose of all mankind.
So, I sat all morning on his window sill, watching
the rain fall, a horse stuck with an overturned

tumbrel wrapped around its hind legs, the struggle
of a woman to sell her rotten potatoes to beggars,
and the sense that time passing meant nothing

at all to anyone except God who knew how it
would all work out and wanted to see if the game
could be played by the rules he set, and how

the outcome of his dreams and planning like
so many prayers offered up in moments when
he was distracted or simply working on something

larger such as the moon, the stars, or the question
of love, could resolve itself as a mathematician
reaches the logical conclusion of a problem only

to see something more stunning, more beautiful,
more trying and defeating in the breadth of answers.
And then, as if it had all come down to this,

the Angelic Doctor pulled the pin, and I danced
on its painful eternity, knowing that had I flesh
or bread within me, it would come to naught

and the only answer possible would be suffering.
The rose fell to the floor. The summer outside
was eaten alive by time. The students learned

and grieved at all they knew when it could not
save them from the depth of their own fears;
but I held the answer—a single time and place,

a single being in a single moment with my right
foot on the impaling edge of the world, and my
left arm raised to heaven holding it there in balance.

Focaccia

Rosemary is for remembrance,
its needles breathe the scent of pine
after an autumn rain

and dipped in olive oil or spread
with the last remaining crumbs of light
remember the taste of summer.

I know I can never write a poem
to pry a fresh warm piece from you.
You make it better than words.

Lammas Bannock

In the mind it is only midsummer—
the apparitions of water dancers
skittering on the channel, late afternoon,

the sun tanning flat limestone slabs
as they heat enough to bake bread.
But inside each tree, inside each

bird and breathing thing that sings
for a life it can never swallow,
inside the belly of the sun, there is

never enough life to feed
the joy of living; so the days grow
elderly until they no longer

feed themselves. Imagine wintering
here past the first snows. November
grows old too. Your love for time

turns to pity. The channel hardens
to a mirror where beauty is inveterate.
The first week's batch of pioneer zeal—

chopping wood and stoking the fire—
sweetens your spirit of northern hardiness;
but soon it becomes a story that will

never stop telling itself, and you just
want it to end. When it does, the world
is old and blind with only stars to guide it

and it curls into itself, its open mouth
in the shape of a prayer, to live again.
Part of you wants to believe life

is born through sleeping mouths, the way
a rumour turns into a legend or taste
becomes a craving too remote to satisfy—

and as you look across to Wikwemikong
where no one ever sets a camp
or hauls down the tattered warrior flag

that has hung like a fool's vision quest
for the past seven years, you see
a woman bent, a black kettle beside her,

a fire trailing smoke into September sky,
a seductress in a cloud's chemise:
she is clapping bannock as she pauses

because she knows you are watching her
in your binoculared distance, knows
you imagine what she is making.

Bread on Water

It is harder to tell the difference
between my kayak paddle dipping
and my hand trailing in the current
as the afternoon grows timeless...

fingers and waters ringing them
are cool in the tall reflected nimbi
sprouting reeds at ease so gracefully
among red wings on rushed banks.

Slice and flash of sunlit droplets,
the silver paddle song is not a lie,
as momentarily our strokes unison
until you leave me in my time.

Turning far downstream, the dam
mumming the flow, you call to me—
something of my grandmother's lilt
echoes like decades in your girlhood.

I see myself on the *Thomas Rennie*,
pulsing across Toronto Harbour,
the city shrinking like a cowardly crowd.
My Nana scatters crusts for the ducks.

By the time we reach the still lagoons,
interwoven like fingers in a handclasp
of mirrored willows on Algonquin Island,
she's struck a truce between the season

and time's untenable liquid flow,
calling only to vanish in perfect pitch,
the Irish in her voice fading to silence,
as my kayak edges softly into yours,

and the sky in the Kagawong River
opens to uphold you as if a yellow bird,
the wings of our paddles almost clasped,
as we drift together until I let you go.

Marcus Aurelius in the Tranquility Garden

Bread have I none, yet still I cleave to reason.

—MEDITATIONS

A fountain should not live by lily pads
or burbling waters alone, nor bravery
in winter when crust ice weighs itself
on the shoulders of encircling walls
that bear the indignity of peanut shells;
for stoicism is made for lesser things,
for birds that drink as if they were dust
or passions of peeling birches waiting
for a love of lesser things to blossom...

for Time, the philosopher would argue,
is measured in mornings that promise
the day will be a day of change and all
the temporal calm will have to reconcile
itself to passages of old men who come
and go and feed the squirrels and never
repent their absence when they are gone
with a chuckle of bread crumbs on paths
or birdsong to mark the sparrow's grave.

Macarons

I am delighted
when you

are delighted
by the way

things have
of working out—

how you sat
on my knee

one Saturday
in your twos

and pointing
to a picture

of the Eiffel Tower
said simply *Paris.*

I have been
but a small part

of the world
that has become

your life
and what little

gift I gave
to you

you baked
into a city

brilliant
with your light.

The Manitoulin Book of the Dead

I have given you the life of the spirit in place of bread
  and water
And a contented heart instead of bread and beer
                              —AMEN-EM-HAT *BOOK OF THE DEAD*, ROM

1.

As you sweep the final crumbs from the table
and the last guests have departed into silence

and emptiness of over-baked banana bread
suffers the exhaustion of oft repeated narrative

where you spoke of what I did during those days
when life passed by thinking I was already gone,

I will be standing by you, longing to show you
what I have discovered in the land of far away.

My feet will be wet from the waters that washed
my soul clean as I set forth on my new journey,

and I will look at the floor behind me but see only
the familiar pattern on the carpet, the boards

of the stair that no longer creak beneath my weight,
and steps only the dog hears but chooses to ignore.

I will whisper something in your ear meant for love,
but like so much of love is better felt than heard.

2.

What first surprised me was the way eel grass
glistened as if it had been born in diamonds

after rain or an early morning damp that clung
to every leaf and sinew of green brilliance

with the shimmering of Jay Creek in sunlight.
I followed the stream, wondering if the source

was pure and full of life, remembering the way
water could spring from rock if thirst was great.

I came upon a small cataract over stones
worn smooth with the wisdom of fidelity

and realized that the water was not falling
but flowing upwards towards its origin because

the path to understanding oneself is the path
of return, and I knew I had been here before.

Ironwood leaves that might have turned to parchment
on the ground were rising among the branches

and reattaching themselves to their lost hopes
as if bare arms of the offshoots were offering alms.

A dead limb overhung the waterfall and as
I touched it with my hand it sang into blossom.

3.

Do not think I have descended into the silence
that chokes whispers as if snowfall at midnight.

Do not think I walk in darkness when night
has given up its frenzy to a depth beyond dreaming

where dawn has been lost so long it cannot
be remembered with either desire or satisfaction.

I am walking in a place where the warblers awoke
hours before I arrived here, where aubades

were given up in gratitude to stars for their
constancy when love was almost beyond recall

and only love's memory guided my soul forward.
The moment that never changes around me

reminds me of all the other passages I learned
through the hardship of grief without realizing

only tears came from those who could not
see beyond where they stood, a moment's blindness.

I return to that moment when I said goodbye
to my father behind the cemetery chapel,

when I thought I should never see him again;
yet I anticipate his face around every turn,

in every sparkle in the brook's bright waters,
in the rustling of every leaf upon every tree

as the wind touches them and speaks of truth;
or the lowering of my grandfather into the fall earth

as the ash cross caught the wind and abandoned
the trust we placed in the philosophies of God

scattering the ritual of his dust into September
and saying there is only permanence in hope.

If I could tell you that I have found God's island
and I am certain I am walking a sure pathway

to the source of the Manitou River, you would not
shed a tear for anyone, but only join them

in a chant of hope you hear in the sound
of a kingfisher searching for its lost mate.

Look into the wind with me now. See the designs
of our belief floating there—the dust from my

grandfather's burial, the smoke from my father's
passage into forever, and the footsteps I leave

with you as a key to unlock the door you find
as I wait for you to join me on this island.

4.

Let me comfort you with the failure of all my
worldly knowledge, for I should only know

such failure when I kneel beside that brook,
cup the waters in my hand, and drink deeply.

All the prayers I ever offered up to heaven
are but crumbs on the table of divinity now.

All the poems I ever wrote are but the taste
of a banquet long after the world has become

hungry again with the ache inside for words,
that insatiable need for something new.

This other world is not unlike the last one.
It is a place where I dream of writing more,

where I need not offer prayers for certainty
and take in every second of what I see

before it fades from the fingertips of memory.
This is a place where I must make something,

where I must shape the clay beneath my feet,
where I must read the landscape as a new book.

I know now that I leave nothing behind me,
that I carry with me the knowledge that keeps

asking me to know more even though I might
be learning everything and seeing everything

in a momentary glimmer of fractured sunlight.
But regardless of all I have known, it passes,

and as in the world I left behind me, forgets
not only itself but all who know it until it is nameless.

I have brought books with me to this island,
and their pages crumble in the spirit of my hands.

I brought pens and paper with me so I could account
the miraculous birds and flowers and remember

them all if it should pass away; and when I reached
for them, they were nowhere to be found,

the warblers, the ironwood—nowhere except in words
made from the prayers I whispered in life.

Making and unmaking is as certain as eating bread,
and I have arrived here, eaten, and am still hungry.

5.

So, I ask myself what was I in that realm of where
and when as time rolled over us in its great deceit

and we were as helpless in its hands as sorrow?
What made us hold on through winters and days

when we never understood the fire that moved
within us as we stared at constellations and thought

they were of something different than ourselves?
Have you ever dreamed of knowing contentment

as you stood on a busy corner waiting for the light
to move you forward as if it was a call for love?

Have you woken in the night and felt that hunger
deep within you and gone to the window knowing

that something in the snow or pages of falling
leaves on a rainy night was alive and burning

to tell you the secret of peace you have kept
within you from the moment of your birth?

It is there, my love. It speaks across great distances
with the passion of a wanderer who must return

to you in moments of stillness, carrying a heart,
a candle, a whisper, a gentle touch you cannot

feel, to reassure you, to offer you that shimmering
of mornings you have not yet known, the word

that far beyond anything you have dreamed
we shall be comforted by a clan of mergansers.

6.

Here is an offering of bread I place before the mouth
of one who cannot eat the knowledge of this world.

It is the bread a stranger offers when he knows
how little you have eaten. It is the sacrifice you made

every day of life, he tells you, as he beckons you
to the table where a meal is spread before you

and there will be time enough later to eat it all.
I sit there as the son of my parents and all before

who led me to this momentary grace of reassurance.
We are not judged because we hunger, but because

we have not fed others; and we are forgiven such
for here, no one shall go without. There is plenty.

I shall say the blessing as I sit at my ancestors' feast,
a short prayer of thankfulness, head bowed, at table

again after such a long time; and happiness
shall be ours when the loaf is broken at last.

I shall save a place for you. We shall sit together
as we lived together, having never left you through all.

7.

I am still with you though the house is empty.
A lover cannot abandon what he loves most.

You will think of the day the rain fell softly
on the cottage roof and we sat in silence reading

the old books we found waiting on the shelves.
All I have said here is what was written in mine.

When I finished, I returned it quietly to its shelf.
It is waiting there in the peace of a summer day,

its pages still bearing the imprint of my fingers,
and hands with which I pledged my faith to you.

After you have sat in silence and emptied your grief
into those places where we consign time past

and things that are no longer part of our lives,
I shall feed on those last crumbs upon our table,

reassemble them as a loaf for us to eat some day
when you shall join me in the place beyond desire.

I shall prepare a table for you there, a banquet
where we taste the moments we knew our joys,

the seconds that stand perfectly still like summer,
waiting for us there, to sustain our truest selves.

Bread: A Mass for Voices
at the Winter Solstice

Panis angelicus
Fit panis hominum
Dat panis coelicus
Figuris terminum
O res mirabilis
Manducat Dominum
Pauper, pauper
Servus et humilis

Introit & Kyrie: Risen

Coming down off Jerusalem Hill,
we could see the North Channel
reaching inland to Honora Bay
as if offering us its life blood.
What sustains our spirits comes
in smaller packages—the glint
of sunlight off a barn's tin roof,
swoops of dragonflies in our path,
the scent of warm bread we imagine.

There was a bakery in Spring Bay
where the incense of risen life sang
like April in our noses and mouths
as we stood by the shop's screen door—
the kind of bread that gives itself up,
fresh and freely, a dusting of snow
still covering its tanned brown skin
as if it had known our condition
and withstood it with kindness.

Guided by that distant light, hungry,
waiting for what we believed to be
the truth of bread, the very breadness
we had craved so long in our cores,
we found the bakery gone. A cock
crowed in the distance, may have
been crowing all day as if to awaken
the endless dead, a cliché of silence
no metaphor answers except by miracle.

It was too late now in the afternoon
to go back home and make our own.
The whiteness of the loaf rose
and rode behind us in the east,
a ghostly shadow still abiding us,
attempting to befriend and sustain
the way no bun or cracker ever could.
And so, we floated on God's island
sailing, somewhere, on blue water;

and talked about what would have been,
the way we remembered what used to be,
how early on late winter mornings
when prayers hovered before our eyes
and the crunch of crust underfoot
was an act of loving devotion in step
with simple desires, we would open
the door, a bell would ring, and there
as if by magic, something we believed in.

Let us remember the mercy we tasted,
the way summer afternoons shine on us
and make us hunger as if the light above
is stretched out inside us and calls us
to that place in ourselves where we find
forgiveness from the pain of simple desire.
Let us remember the mercy of fresh bread,
how it called to us in our imaginations
even after it ceased to be and lived on inside.

Confession: Manet's Boule

après Le Déjeuner sur l'herbe

As in herbaceous dreams
where one is playing cello
or naked in a concert hall
and the sheet music is lost
or the words are missing,

I dreamed of afternoons—
unmistakably cruel dreams—
deep in a shaded forest
where a young woman,
so casually and candidly,

stares in blithe delight
as if she wore nothing
but the beauty of ideas
and not great ones at that.
I gave up such dreaming

by the time I'd graduated
and the frame had shrunk
the way an afternoon ends
with a dusky bifocal vision—
evening spread before me

and the mortgaged house
a tomb I need to conquer
before Hades locks me in.
I can just afford a basket
of pink Ontario peaches,

friends of easy leisure,
a bottle to wash down time,
and cherries I can suck on
as art evolves beyond me
like that overgrowing forest

rife with blissful *étrangers*
in fitted birthday suits.
I miss those days I never
had, the simple beauty
of wasted youth. Instead,

I hung over archives—
the best hours of my life—
when others were making
love or discovering how
much joy meant to them

on afternoons in groves
of sacred trees where artists
flirted with the shadows,
catching glimpses of flesh,
its miraculous bread-like light.

Times instead I puzzled
at solving puzzles where
pieces remained lost and I
skipped lunches in the quad
to read a few pages more

as others sat and listened
to the remains of Nature
enchanting them to dreaming.
But in Manet's soft *maniera*
of couples in the woods,

a sylvan afterthought comes
to me like a formal feeling
or an offering from gods—
his boule hovers temptingly
at the canvas's lower edge

as if he is saying *it is yours*
I know your appetite, a hunger
deep inside you that never
will be fed—and as I reach
to take it, the dog barks,

the telephone rings—yet I
know the taste of sourdough
when it's fresh, unregretful,
as if just born in paradise,
something from long ago,

untouched by human hands
or the gaze of the woman there
whose eyes to me are music,
an instrument I have mastered,
a part I have learned to play.

God forgives those tempted
by the knowledge of life unlived,
but not art, alas, not art.
The round boule in the foreground
is still waiting to be tasted.

Gloria: Jacob's Pillow

I take it bread
is the substance
of dreams,

that together as
we lay our heads
it answers desire

with a passing
prayer, a hunger
for what was.

I take it this is
the way to heaven,
a ladder of loaves

our spirits climb,
pillow of glory
a scone of stone

to crown desires—
O fill my head
with passing dreams,

the glories of loss
the fears of love...
Rise into the night

and let us feed.
We make heaven
from crumbs of life.

If I told you
over morning toast
last night the angels

climbed my thoughts
you would tell me
to go back to sleep.

Gradual: Shopping Cart

All the foods I am about to consume
stare at me like panthers in their cage,
and through chrome bars and Rilke eyes
study me and wild, unchosen shelves.

A neighbour waves, her basket brimful.
She celebrates the pleasure of the kill.
The Vidalias in her child care carrier
will make her weep tonight for beauty.

I am going to hold a funeral for food,
remember kindly all it did for me;
years spent torturing a Brussels sprout,
or crusts, a great heart, beneath a plate.

Allelluia: Cinnamon Buns

You gave me a copy of *Life* to play with,
the cover featuring two bald old men,
Vienna, late 1950s,
settling, or so it seemed,
the evils of the modern world.
I thought all things were run by elves.

They lived in the nether regions of Kresge's
where trays of steaming cinnamon buns
emerged hot and sticky on the hour,
filling the crowded baked-goods counter
(even the cheap notions department)
with the opiate smell of eternal hope.

They came to symbolize what we were,
kings of tomorrow, bourgeois kitchens,
islands of sugar, cinnamon, endless talk.
Some declared they could die for them.

Though they were never half as good cold,
the world was cold, and war was cold,
and butter couldn't melt in our mouths
except if a single raw flash of light
exploded the boundary between us and them.

Credo: The Temptation of Bread

Forgive me what I do not know,
about the way knowledge feeds

and yet after leaves one hungry,
how a life of sustenance is only

known by the need to eat again
the sourdough bread of ideas.

Forgive that I've been deceived
by knowledge, by what I know

and its satisfaction, take this bread
and use it wisely. If I am left

with questions, then I am fed.
If I am fed, there are more to come.

I have no answers but desire only
the temptation of an empty mouth.

Liturgy: Visiting P.K.

> *There is a woman floating in a window*
> *Transparent*
> *Christmas wreaths in passing houses*
> *Shine now in eye and now in hair, in heart.*
>
> —P.K. PAGE, "Reflection in a Train Window"

There is a woman floating in a window,
and light through Venetian blinds
transforms her into bars of music,
mystical and almost transparent.
Do you like Philip Glass, she asks?
Victoria buried by a sudden snow,
her garden city is a Christmas world.
The kettle boiled, she wets the tea
and through steam and filigree shadow
there is a woman floating in a window.

Transparent—
that is the word I want to give to her,
the way light makes poetry of her face,
the eyes that remind me of an icon,
hair that reflects the soft voice of angelic
nuances hidden in language crafted with an accent
that echoes to the dithyrambic turnings

of Glass music filling the house
like wind chimes making the dissonant
transparent—

Christmas wreaths in passing houses
my cab passed on the way here this day
are lifebuoys in a sea of sudden snows
and not entirely out of place among
her thoughts on poetry: we talk of *Preview*,
Patrick Anderson, Judith Cape, the muses
of Modern verse, and where retired
inspirations go as if a poet ever said no
to what she could hold on to; seasons, causes,
Christmas wreaths in passing houses...

Shine now in eye and now in hair, in heart
that memory should set you in the window there,
a winter sun making you even more serene,
more of what I remember now—the snow—
flecking your steel-grey hair, shining
trees bent beneath their weight, the subtle start
to a new year, perhaps another poem.
Thank God memory is an ageless place
like the inside of a glosa. Let the art
shine now in eye and now in hair, in heart.

Purification: Gingerbread House

Overhanging the eaves
a white lip of fondant
almost wants to smile

as you press gumdrops
around the door to light
a path for travellers.

It's always snowy winter
for houses of gingerbread.
A dusting of icing sugar

over a printless threshold
suggests they sleep inside
or, hard at work baking,

mix lives with stories
that soon are eaten up.
It's a good day to stay in,

to put a roof over dreams,
keep them warm, protect
them from passing storms,

let rise a breath of incense,
as you draw a pan of walls
from the open smile you feed.

A Reading from the Gospel of Lauro de Bosis

As he banked over the Casa San Angelo,
the roof tiles below were a sea of blood

and the dark avenues and arteries coursed
with a pulsing hunger that could not be fed.

Bread to a starving city, he thought
and the leaflets proclaiming Fascism's end

fluttered whitely in his wake like doves.
They shall be devoured, but the word is spoken.

The fashionable parties could say nothing;
hallways where officials knew him well were mute;

but up here, beyond the domes and illusions,
beyond the very fingertips of futile history

he was rising and shining in his silver plane
and the spirit of freedom settled to the ground.

Bread to a starving city, he had written,
and turning once over the Coliseum's shell,

one dip-winged pass before heading to death,
he saw the arms upraised and feeding,

catching every crumb his spirit rained down,
and realized the masses had received the word,

and history took his body up as prayer.
Come into his house and eat your fill;

there is much of the world you hunger for;
make your table a place of nations.

Offertory: Hot Cross Buns

To live is to give up loved things—
a bird, a meal, a remembered day;
the spirit of life only living brings.

My childhood pet had yellow wings
and poured out its song as if to say
to live is to give up loved things.

No warm hands, no admonishings
caged its breath as it slipped away...
the spirit of life only living brings.

My voice keened with sobbings
to answer the depths of February:
living I gave up such loved things

for the bread of Lenten offerings,
currants, raisins, fruit hidden away.
The spirit of life only living brings

feeds me, though I cannot fill my cravings,
can only exclaim *in manus tuus domine:*
to live is to give up loved things,

to endure flights of fancy, stilled wings,
motionless among crusts and mystery,
the spirit of life only living brings.

First death and last are but beginnings—
of what, only time and faith can say.
Though to live is to give up loved things,
the spirit is love and the bird still sings.

Eucharist

If I say I need you to survive
there must be life in what rises here—
blood, body, all it means to be alive.

Time and love are the currency of life—
as they dwindle they grow more dear
if I say I need you to survive.

Charity is to give all one has to give—
here is my spirit, my heart, my ear,
blood, body, all it means to be alive,

for we come through winters to thrive
on a promise, married by love, not fear
because I said I need you to survive.

The world began with such a promise I've
made each day we eat at our table here:
blood, body, all it means to be alive

and the insatiable, impatient hunger I give
to you and you to me all in the name of love,
blood, body, all it means to be alive,
if I say I need you to survive.

Sanctus: Bread

Let us proclaim the mystery of bread,
how it breathes life even as it melts,
how it is like spring because it rises
from the hands of its maker's sleep
and becomes itself in a crucible of warmth.

Let us proclaim the sacrifice of crusts,
how the shell forms upon the outer loaf,
how it hardens as it lives and learns
and is broken only when you hunger,
giving itself lovingly for the love of others.

Let us proclaim the necessity of love,
how it is a question that is never answered,
how it is eaten as you would a wish
and swallowed as you would a prayer,
so it is never answered until you know it is.

Let us proclaim the faith of bread,
how it satisfies with love and sacrifice,
how it only sustains when it is shared
and is tasted when it must be tested.
Break it open. It is in you to eat.

Prayer: The Domestication of Bread

I believe that bread was never wild,
but there was a time it grew on trees;
or rather, hung from branches temptingly,
hot and enticing with the aroma of God,
aching for butter, its innards steaming.
This, we said, was divinity in sustenance.

Some said it needed wine, a red
to wash the bitterness down. Others
declared that water was the cure,
the Spartan pride that gaolers have
for their answer to hunger and our ills.
When it wasn't there, we understood loss.

Clever ones said they'd make their own,
raise the grain, eat of the earth,
but the truth of bread was slain with a bone
and when skies grew empty, so did our souls;
so we invented the very means of knowing.
When knowledge failed, we learned to question.

Could find its scent throughout the house,
the air wafting with a call to praise—
the women singing as flat loaves rose,
the men waiting because love is a hunger
and children pressing against the door
asked if miracles could happen sooner.

This is how we brought joy to our lives—
not that we need what bread could teach us,
but because it was something so familiar—
celebration that pointed the way to dreaming,
the need that woke us to find ourselves,
and mornings we prayed and loaves ballooned.

In every loaf there is a message hiding,
though in truth we never pause to read it.
You can taste it when the bread is gone.
It is a simple statement about desert lands,
how in baked horizons when the feet are sore
there is water in stones and tomorrows in sunsets.

Agnes Dei: Flouring

The lawn today is barely dusted,
whitened just enough to seem mature,
wearing its age with autumnal grace,
a pale sprinkling in the subtle dawn
the way my mother dusted a board,
flouring it before delving in dough,
her fingers not unlike a tree's boughs
as they shaped, swam and squeezed.

The flouring was for giving back—
after the mixture had been tidily worked
the board would release it, a promise
kept, a bond upheld. Baking was honour.
In the world of an unrisen crust
faces of friends and family past
would crack and emerge like echoes
when the mound endured her work—

noses, chins, loving familiar eyes,
visions of momentary reappearance,
shades of memories ever changing
until the narrative between her hands
had given up its legends to silence
and the next batch was up to us.
My daughter writes her footprints
in the snowy yard. A new chapter begins.

Let me work my part as she works
the tracery of a moment white in breath,
a map of myths we tell ourselves
because the telling, not the story,
is what keeps us fed on daily bread,
forgiving our trespasses as we
forgive those who disappeared in time,
remembered quietly in the falling snow.

Dismissa: Injera

for Zewde and Abebe

The world is a language of bread
and our mouths open to speak it.
It is warm flesh beneath fresh *wat*,
the sensual *berbere* on our hands:
a morsel but a mouthful for a king.

This is how Solomon once fed,
keeping his belly full of royal wit
and offering wisdom as he sat
in glory dreaming of scented lands
that gave love a richer meaning.

Kef fermenting as if long dead
reminded him of wine, the poet
in him hungering for a love that
fed on likenings and lilies and
honey, the purity in a holy thing.

The prison where they kept you did
not hold you though on release it
left you without those at the *wat*
who dipped a brotherly hand
into the plate we are now sharing.

This meal is where dreams lead
when the world cannot acquit
others of their wrongs, and yet
we forgive them because it stands
to reason we are not yet dying.

What sustains us is not bread
but the work, the cooking, the *fitfit*
red as a sacrifice, the afterthought
of food and conversation, the bonds
between the hungry, the quiet eating,

the memory of what was said,
stories that time and dinners knit
as if a cloth woven from the chat
that warms us and helps us understand
what sharing is as we go on living.

III

The Bread of Angels: A Spring Canticle

We answer hunger with the reassurance of bread
because nothing so reflects the spirit
of our true natures.
—JACQUES MARITAIN

Montreal Bread Company

I sought my beloved in the wilderness
    where the loaves remain unleavened
        as mighty roads; she was not there.

I called her name to the dying waves
    and the salt spray touched me
        with the tears of an exile's desire—

and even in the labyrinth of forests
    where the hard earth rose in loaves
        and twisted themselves in hard tack

until they fell like leaves in the pity
    of ageless beauty and grew tired
        with soft green lichen for a bed—

I sought her and she was not there.
    O sisters among the shadows of the city—
        do you know where my beloved sleeps?

Will you comfort me with espressos
    when midmorning melts the noonday sun
        and somewhere crows still shadow her eyes?

Will you offer me biscotti as my solace
        and if I dip it in the soul of rain will the sweetness
            of her sugared kiss come to me in jazz?

A Last Cake of Snow

The spring air is the flavor
of icing sugar melting away
on the budded tips of tongues—

that edge where cautious words
such as *long* and *labour*
linger with citric lemon.

The air is bright today,
the sun rubs itself to warmth again
and an *amuse bouche* of late March

leaves an island on the lawn
not unlike the one that fed us
loaf after loaf in our imaginations—

a miracle for winter voyagers
who journeyed through hard months
that end in perplexing y's.

One lone lemon drop
on the sideboard's cake stand
dares lead us into temptation—

the one last taste of Christmas,
the one we offered over dinner
when we couldn't eat one more...

until one day it simply vanishes
like that island of snow on our lawn
or the recipes for love we lost.

La Giaconda *under the Stove*

After I had stared into her brown eyes
for the better part of an afternoon
and watched as they followed shadows
caught in a nest of kitchen shelves,

I thought *you are home now*, back safely
in your humble roots, in a land not afraid
of the true taste of food; I put her away
under the stove and made a bowl of polenta.

The salt bread of strangers is not beautiful.
Know where you belong and love it dearly.
To be an exile is to live without speaking,
as if tombed in a closet of the Salon Carré

where I waited in darkness to set her free,
testing the patience of the love she speaks
that blindly calls itself art. Over her left
shoulder, where a road turns to the mountains

and an image of the Ponte Vecchio, the Arno
and the unworn hills of Tuscano rise
like fingers to touch the hem of heaven,
a feast awaits to put a smile on her face,

so I laid her down, wrapped as if parmaggiano
in a clean white veil, somewhere warm
out of the sun, wimpled to protect her delicate skin.
Yes. She thanked me with her steady smile.

Talking in My Sleep

Must have been something
I was dreaming just now,

an old song you used to love,
a promise I still intend to keep,

the name of an avenue
or just a fond secret.

If it doesn't make sense,
then it need not make sense.

The truth is the truth
no matter how garbled.

A flower is a flower
even before spring.

I was asking the waiter
for some bread of angels.

Pita Crisp

You stand beside me after school,
snapping crisps like lessons in your hands

reminding me of what I should learn,
will learn, or have forgotten,

the little questions that all add up,
the mystery of crumbs we cannot solve.

Castor Carnivores (Legend of the Werebeaver)

I put out crusts for the werebeaver
knowing it might otherwise feed
on dreams of sleeping children.

In my sleep, it gnaws on bedposts
like a legend of voyageurs or mad
trappers who ran the woods and lost

control in labyrinths of plenty.
I see its evil handiwork in hills
that dam up rivers or ox-bow scars

meanderings fed into frigid lakes
where artists drown, creating
a dark, reflective, mossy place

that has yet to waken from its birth.
I know that a trail of bread crumbs
will coax the creature to its lodge,

that cozy room on winter nights
where it hovers over its sleeping wife,
turns away in wakeful dreaming,

and leaves footprints beyond the garden,
topples fragile birches, stick maples,
and breaks the covenant of silence.

It will stop and drink at a dark pool,
recite the poetry of nature sunk
so low in its soul it cannot sing.

The moonlight will reveal its eyes,
blue and star-struck as if still dreaming.
Its mouth will chew and chew on bread

as if wanting to swallow but so afraid
there might be knowledge in what it eats...
that someone in the night is watching...

that someone knows how much it hungers,
where it comes from, and who it is...
that this is how I sustain myself.

Wedding Cake

Wedding cakes are made from ulterior motives,
multi-layered and stacked like generations

of familial memories in photograph albums.
They are sweet for the moment, but last years,

buried deep in freezers or tucked away
beneath pillows for maidens to dream of heroes.

When you cut ours, my hand guiding yours
against the resistance of confectioner's art,

a layer of strawberries leapt heartily to life,
and we knew the life-blood was in our kiss.

＊　＊　＊

In an old glossy photo a half-century grey,
my parents stand beside their wedding cake,

the cake and my mother adorned in pearls,
my father still young and so full of vitality.

Look at their light—they have doves eyes—
soft and shining like a September day, leaves

through the window still held by their trees,
the way life holds on in the face of storms,

saying *here is the food of love we share,*
come take it, sleep on it, and make it yours.

*   *   *

There is wedding cake in the silence years on
when two people can sit in the same quiet room

and be comforted by each other's presence,
the hard icing that keeps freshness in,

decorative rosettes, the doll bride or bell.
What we claim from each other over a lifetime

is assurance that we may always claim more,
and by staking such rights sustain our world,

days yawning with open mouths to feed
the hunger we must answer, so beautiful in white.

Vintage

Though it hurts,
it makes sense—
this cruel fusion,
blood and bread,

as the knife slips
between my fingers
and the focaccio
reddens as if cut.

Pretend a moment
that fresh blood
is Italian balsamic,
hint of rosemary—

salty to taste,
just slightly metallic,
the illusion of iron
melted quickly away,

a wine cellared
far too long,
lingering with desire
to be consumed,

the sad truth of time
told on deathbeds
those confessions, absolving
the world's sweetness

of complicity, pain,
sorrow of having
a vision of heaven
almost to taste...

Put the wound
to my lips, say
a small prayer,
the angel's portion.

Thin Buns

for Peter McEwen at Owen Sound

Peter aimed the *Moody Blue* at the gemini
his girls had stationed on the family's jetty

to guide us across the dark open channel,
its waters slapping on the metal hull,

sounds of applause for having made
time in the motor boat with only the shade

of a sunset reflecting the face of his island
and its loon-mottled shimmering to hand

us a faint target in the antique twilight.
And when the bright eyes came in sight,

a lantern for each granddaughter there,
he cut the engine; and the sound of water

on rock as if a book someone was flipping
pages in, looking for a word slowly slipping

away, perhaps through a hole in the wall,
could capture succeeding summers and all

the brave suppers alfresco beneath pines
and a blue sky that redoubtably still shines

with perils of winters past and to come,
the tranquility of an island, Peter's home.

Dinner on a cottage deck has the taste
of heaven; sausages in thin buns waste

no bread because here is where everything
must be accounted for, where light harvesting

a cloudless afternoon allows us to see each
other on the porch as we talk and teach

our souls how to simply be. And lying there
in the dark with only the sweet-grass air

to remind the senses of a lantern full moon
and its image echoing off water, too soon

sleep creeps over the barnboard Sound
and reality is a brief dream only loaned

from the depths. Surely, it is a good thing
to believe in happiness, at least reassuring.

Tomorrow is another imaginary July day
and shouts of girlhood splash in Peter's bay.

6th Concession, Tehkummah Township

The car nuzzles into the soft shoulder.
I step across the quickened ditch
embroidered in Queen Anne's lace
lanced with sharpened goldenrod,

and reach a split-rail cedar fence
that snakes like a water moccasin
around the field's serrated edge.
My hand brushes whiskers of wheat.

This year they have planted for bread,
a return of God's grain to God's island
where Cain trod on limestone shelves
and stalks rise from ancient reefs.

Years ago, before gaudy canola
or the fallen sky-blue of pointillist flax,
last Saxon squares of gothic Durum
stood like Maldon men against change.

Doubt and redoubt did the rest; but wheat
is a summons to life and rises when
the world seems without a prayer.
In the sands today at Providence Bay

it was there as Huron heaved its sigh
taking its licks with dune cranberries
and other defiantly delicate flora—
and yesterday at the crop of Fossil Hill

I saw it split the fissured limestone
as if made from poetry's shards,
and it wavered with the ancient corals,
rebirth announced from an open tomb.

Forgiveness is all around me here,
for harsh as it is, this earth cannot hate,
for its love is the love of hardship and bread,
and my slice of lunch loaf, warm as breath,

was there to greet me like a summer's day,
forgiving morning's thunderclap shouts,
the tears that almost drowned the world,
partnered with life toward a common goal;

and each head greening to spread its seeds,
is a supplicant's hands that reach for life,
sharing the secret of our common need,
and the sun—a loaf of fresh, warm bread.

IV

Stone Bread: Summer Plainsong

What is it, mortals, that you hope to gain
from one another?
—PLATO, *THE SYMPOSIUM*

Empire Cookies

Traditions don't die; they just fade
to whispers until all you can hear
is the sound of lake water's charade
lapping the legs of a pant-rolled bather

standing on rock vertebrae at Kagawong
and stretching his pince-nez sight far
into the cloud-struck shore along
the ridge-backed north. Bernard Trotter

built his camp nearby just as the First War
dug into the lengthy spine of Europe;
his name is engraved as a battle scar
in Paris's Pantheon. There was hope

poetry might end the war to end
all wars. Summers and wars later,
my rail-thin niece and daughter send
a stick floating beyond the harbour

with a message *peace* written on its side
in indelible marker. They believe currents
will carry it to the sea and the far side
of the world, to somewhere somnolent

in the charred dark. During our picnic,
they cram Empire cookies in their faces,
fondant like a shell over a plaque
of shortbread crumbs that erases

another vestige of a past we choose
to swallow without thinking of pity.
So where is Bernard's camp? So close
to this it could almost be a mystery.

I shall spend an evening drinking whisky
by fire beneath the crumbling stars,
and in that moment retrieve what echoingly
once was human and should still be ours.

The worldly spheres the two girls love
are ghost-white with icing and a cherry moon,
and the sun never sets while flagging above
hovers a maw to devour it too soon.

Crackers

Lying in bed on a summer night
and listening to the rain falling
on my life to wash all the light
from the stars, I consider my calling.

Stupidity or courage are matters
where one does the wrong thing
until, when everything is tatters,
it becomes right and the suffering

seems justified. I am an idiot.
There are crumbs in this bed.
My life is a loaf I made out
of the grain I grew and had

to feed my family. Was it the right
thing? Did I miss a train somewhere
and arrive at the wrong place bright
and early but with nothing there

except some vague idea that things
would work out if I let them? The rain
has stopped. It is dark. A daft bird sings,
never to know if he could live his life again.

Vanishing Cream

in memory of Amy Winehouse

At Wevill's house one desert night
as I lay reading at the window screen,
a moth flew into my lit candle
and fell burning like a torch song.

By the time I snuffed the flame,
wondering if any art was worth
a life—even a dumb insect's—
only the wings' eyes remained.

I watched other moths, less talented,
dance and beat themselves helpless
against the metal mesh, their flutters
the sound of an old film projector

running silent movies, unaccompanied,
the movements of faces overplayed,
each pancaked to reflect a light
shining through them to the future.

My grandmother would remove her face
each night before she went to sleep
with a cream that made her ghostly,
letting the day vanish as if a miracle—

the same way I thought nature sang
when I woke at dawn to uneasy steps,
my face still pressed against the screen
and a doe's eyes staring back at me.

Supreme Heat

Do your feet sink into doughy asphalt?
Is a shimmering lake on the road ahead?

Can you smell your neck skin as it simmers?
Will you drink an iceberg until it melts as snow?

How can you stand there waiting in the sun?
Why is your hatband reflecting dark thoughts?

Are you sure you have enough salt in your soul?
Does the sound of a cicada measure your pulse?

Shall we lie together without even touching?
Must something always be ready to rise?

Where is a raindrop when a flower is dying?
Who can tell time when stars are burning?

Have you tasted bread when your mouth is dry?
When will the breeze give me back your smile?

Bread for Beginners

Imagine the once-cobbled streets of Paris.
Outside the elegant café rain is falling.
It begins with hunger. That's all it is.

Centuries of famine fade like a kiss.
Lovers in the Catacombs are calling:
Imagine the once-cobbled streets of Paris.

It is always harvest where bread is.
Starvation seems far away, and rain is falling.
It begins with a darkening. That's all it is.

Summers now bring tourists who whiz
past like ghosts on Vespas calling:
Imagine the once-cobbled streets of Paris!`

Watch the boulevards as someone walks his
dog or kisses his girl. Such appalling
history began with hunger. That's all it was.

Stay awake. History is a nightmare. It is.
You insist it is. A beautiful rain is falling.
Imagine the once-cobbled streets of Paris,

a loaf of bread, a child's face, life the size
of pain, a loaf of *pain*. The rain is falling
on imagined streets of a once-cobbled Paris.
A child carries a baguette. That's all it is.

Stone Bread

As I sang Evensong in Gloucester Cathedral,
the croned oak choir stalls with misericords
had been crafted to bear the singer or fall
shut with a deafening bang. Mercy's words
rang through the tongue of a litany's sparks
of Latin that ritualized my dreams. One part
miserly as Misery Bay's beach with marks
of striation grooves, etchings of glacial art;
the other half, Ovid's tender word *cordis*
where the vein of a ring digit runs directly
to the heart for heavenly visions or a promise
of fidelity beyond death or winters, the mercy
that is both hunger and food. On my island,
stone fingers offer waves a Samaritan's hand.

The Latin for mercy is shadowed with misery,
the knowledge we come by through December
and the dark harrowing of nights so snowy
we cannot see the hope of our hands there
to touch something warm and living.
It is summer now as I stand at Misery
Bay. It is possible to see just how forgiving
the world can be with a little possibility—
to say that rock is boule-shaped or a stone
is a stone's throw from an angel's pillow
of chiabata. When poetry ceases, we're alone
with our own despair and the silence, like snow,
can kill us, leaving only the hard crust,
a few windswept crumbs of supper dust.

Can I remember, as a child, hiding my crusts
beneath the edge of the supper plate because
remains kept me from the future? It must
have been the lure of summer as the cause
of it, the thought of cool, warm water between
my toes, or the long day's sigh in humid breath
like a dog that wandered back unseen
into the woods when sunsets like death
crept to the window sill and peered ferociously
to remind me that in China a boy just my age
was going to bed hungry—
and a pang like a zooed animal in the rib cage
ached with guilt, wanting to feed and know him
with more than bread crusts or summer or sin.

As if the liturgy of the personal had been
as easy as breaking bread at dawn, the story
has had the author it deserves—words clear
and plainly put as stones in a sunlit shallow bay
where the Great Spirit made his mark long ago
shaping every morsel to remind a passerby
that part of what we eat is imaginary, ergo,
stone bread...The baker's art of a lived life I
could not have given rise to in my hungering—
wife, daughter, dog, a stone island at the end
of time as I know it by heart, a rendering
of shore grass, sun-baked erratics, a bend
in the shoreline beyond the limits of the mind—
melts in my mouth leaving its mercy behind.

A Ghazal Made Entirely of Dough
for Katie

A handprint white upon your face,
you sift ingredients into place.

A year ago, you would have shaped
animals in dough, but time escaped.

A web forms between your fingers
and beneath your nails flour lingers.

I marvel—the child I partially made
is feeding me with homemade bread.

Light that arrives like a kitchen guest
reveals your earnestness at its best.

Your hair, bun-tied behind each ear
is the colour of loaves I make disappear.

Here an ancient ancestral recipe,
the patience one tastes but cannot see;

for what is sifted, shaped, filled with air,
is the joy of creating what wasn't there.

What rises up must be brought down
for the maker makes the bread her own.

Rosemary is for remembrance. You adorn
the top with memories of our garden.

Your floured hands, first communion gloves,
your fingerprints buried in the loaves,

you make a braid for the top the way
you do your hair on a rainy day;

for having sepulchered them off to bake
you begin again for beginning's sake,

and cut them with a saw-toothed knife,
as you open another door to life.

Dinner Roll
for Kerry

And when one of them finds his other half, whether he
be a lover of youth or a lover of another sort, the pair
are lost in an amazement of love and friendship and
intimacy, and one will not be out of the other's sight,
as I may say, even for a moment...
    —PLATO, *The Symposium*

I love to watch how you
select one from the basket

the way an egg charmer
coddles an Easter surprise.

And as you curl your hand
around its global girth

as if to say the whole world
is there in your warm palm,

I know what it is to love;
to be with you for a meal.

When you broke it open,
I saw how our love tried

to fill the void between
each half, each body now

separate as if miles apart.
I wake in a distant city.

Lights in the window
are unfamiliar. The bed

still holds my body's shape,
a crescent where your teeth

have bitten off the better half.

Pain au Chocolat

To live in a time of miracles
means nothing, though to love
in a time of wonder is what calls
us to this world. Today, above

the Xin'an River in Central China,
a phantom city floated in the mist,
its buildings and towers an enigma
as real as if I turned and kissed

you good morning as you set
a chocolate croissant before me
to dip in my coffee and forget
what the world will do in the melee

of truth and imagination. Beyond
the table and our garden, I believe
I see another realm that dawned
the instant our lips touched to relieve

the silence of loss where love lives.
That world is phantom hope, contains
the secrets of how the chocolate gives
itself to the pastry and yet remains

despite the hunger of an oven's heat,
the separation of delicate layers
that rise into a beautiful truth. Great
things come to those who ask great prayers.

From the Earth to the Moon

The sound of blasting at first light
shakes our glasses beside the bed.
I thought a war had begun or earth
was finally throwing in her towel,
perhaps the wet one you were wearing
as you stepped out of the shower.

I have heard one day bells will ring
after a blast from an angel's horn.
The mountains will all tumble down
and valleys will be raised high. Seas
will peneplain whatever's left.
The world as we know it is so uneven.

I pull aside the blackout drapes.
Everything seems so naked here.
Having checked in to the motel late,
we inherit the damage darkness leaves.
A stand of birches trembles on rock,
and beyond, the stack at Coppercliff.

But your beauty is lunar as you dress.
Your glowing flesh, the silver of thighs,
that startled look from another blast—
bread-white of birches against black stone.
Your slacks are green, your blouse billows,
and things are filled with life again.

You've told me you are from this place,
how your family worked the deepest seams,
growing like trees when trees stopped growing,
always giving back though never giving up.
I stand in the shower and let rain fall.
I am less a stone each time we touch.

Woman Baking Bread

after a painting by Jean François Millet

The heat irons her green work smock
as she squares herself to the glowing door
to test her loaf, and sees it is good

the way an artist bent over newly baked
stars as they cooled with the aroma
of sudden beauty for famished minds.

This is not about work or even hunger,
but about the eye studying deeply
what the hand and heart have done,

the question, *Will it ever be enough*?
There is no satisfaction in a prophet's mouth.
Her oven sings to an impossible God.

Acknowledgements

"Woman Baking Bread" was a finalist in the James Hearst Poetry Prize and appeared in *The North American Review*.

"Gingerbread House," "Dinner Roll," and "Bread on Water," appeared in the anthology *Pith and Wry* edited by Susan McMaster and Roger Nash and published by Your Scrivener Press, Sudbury, Ontario.

"Cinnamon Buns" appeared in the food anthology *Crave It* published by Evergreen Press, Toronto.

"The Domestication of Bread" appeared in *Acta Victoriana*.

"Marcus Aurelius in the Tranquility Garden" appeared in *The Toronto Review*.

"Lammas Bannock," "Summa," "Castor Carnivores," "Vanishing Cream," and "Pain au Chocolat" appeared in *ELQ Magazine (Exile: the Literray Quartelry)*.

The manuscript for *A Book of Bread* received an Ontario Arts Council Works-in-Progress Grant in March of 2011 – the author is grateful for this support. Thanks to Brian Van Noord and the staff of Grenville. The author is grateful to Tim Inkster and Porcupine's Quill Press, Michael Callaghan and Exile Editions, Laurence Steven and Your Scrivener Press, Mike O'Connor and Insomniac Press, Halli Villegas and Tightrope Books for their generous support of this project as it evolved and for Ontario Arts Council Grants provided by the Writers' Reserve Fund. Thanks to Barry Callaghan for supporting my work over the years, and Nina Callaghan for her adroit reader's eye.